Maths at Work

Maths at the Airport

Tracey Steffora

Raintree is an imprint of Capstone Global Library Limited, a company incorporated in England and Wales having its registered office at 7 Pilgrim Street, London, EC4V 6LB – Registered company number: 6695582

To contact Raintree please phone 0845 6044371, fax + 44 (0) 1865 312263, or email myorders@ raintreepublishers.co.uk. Customers from outside the UK please telephone +44 1865 312262.

Text © Capstone Global Library Limited 2013
First published in hardback in 2013
The moral rights of the proprietor have been asserted.

Edited by Dan Nunn and Abby Colich
Designed by Victoria Allen
Picture research by Tracy Cummins
Production control by Victoria Fitzgerald
Printed and bound in China by Leo Paper Products Ltd

ISBN 978 1 406 25071 8
16 15 14 13 12
10 9 8 7 6 5 4 3 2 1

British Library Cataloguing in Publication Data
Steffora, Tracey.
Maths at the airport. – (Maths at work)
510-dc23
A full catalogue record for this book is available from the British Library.

Acknowledgements
We would like to thank the following for permission to reproduce photographs: Alamy: p. 14 (© Jim West); Corbis: pp. 15 (© Robert Maass); dreamstime: p. 21 (Fintastique); Getty Images: pp. 6 (Jupiterimages), 9 (Lester Lefkowitz), 10 (Digital Vision), 11 (Andreas Koerner), 16 (Thinkstock), 18 (Karen Moskowitz), 23a (Jupiterimages); iStockphoto: pp. 5 (© Gene Chutka), 12 (© bojan fatur), 17 (© Gene Chutka), 19 (© mayo5); Shutterstock: pp. 4 (yxm2008), 7 (Remzi), 8 (Lisa S.), 13 (Lars Christensen), 20 (Eric Gevaert), 23b (Eric Gevaert).

Front cover photograph of a pilot sitting at the controls of a commercial aeroplane reproduced with permission from Getty Images/ Digital Vision/ James Lauritz.

Back cover photograph of a ground controller on a runway reproduced with permission from iStockphoto (© mayo5).

The publishers would like to thank Andy Colich for his invaluable help in the preparation of this book.

Every effort has been made to contact copyright holders of any material reproduced in this book. Any omissions will be rectified in subsequent printings if notice is given to the publisher.

Contents

Maths at the airport

Many people work at the airport.

Many people use maths at
the airport.

Counting

flight attendant

The flight attendant counts tickets.

The flight attendant
counts passengers.

baggage handler

The baggage handler counts bags.

How many bags can you count?

(answer on page 22)

Measuring

pilot

The pilot flies the plane.

how fast

The pilot measures how fast the plane is flying.

how high

The pilot measures how high the plane is flying.

plane

tree

Which is higher? The plane or
the tree? (answer on page 22)

Shape and size

The screener looks at bags.

X-ray

The screener looks at the shape
of things inside the bags.

Some bags are large. The flight attendant puts these bags in (16) a locker.

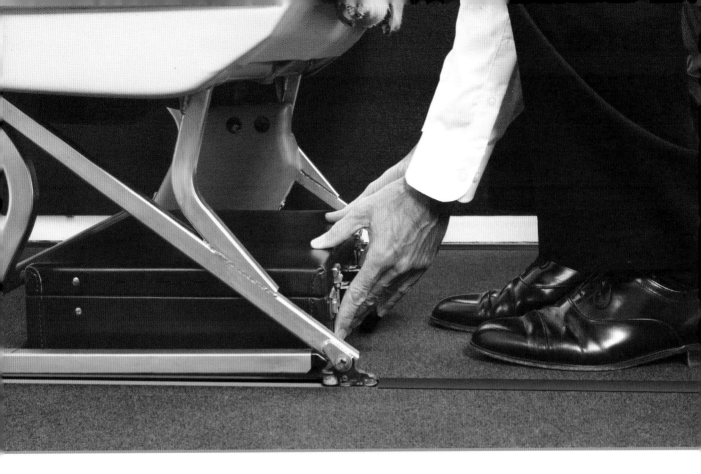

Smaller bags go under the seat.

Is this bag large or small?

(answer on page 22)

Time

ground controller

The ground controller tells a plane when to move.

ground controller

The ground controller tells a plane when to stop.

The air controller tells a plane
when to fly.

DEPARTURES

LOS ANGELES	7:20
SEATTLE	7:40
BOSTON	8:10
CHICAGO	8:30
NEW YORK	9:00
MIAMI	9:15
HOUSTON	9:50
DENVER	10:15

What time does the plane fly to New York? (answer on page 22)

Answers

page 9: There are five bags.

page 13: The plane is higher than the tree.

page 17: The bag is small.

page 21: The plane flies to New York at 9.00.

Picture glossary

ticket paper that shows you have paid for something

air controller person who tells the pilot when to fly the plane

Index

Notes for parents and teachers
Maths is a way that we make sense of the world around us. For the young child, this includes recognizing similarities and differences, classifying objects, recognizing shapes and patterns, developing number sense, and using simple measurement skills.

Before reading
Connect with what children know
Discuss types of transport and identify that one way we can travel is by aeroplane. Allow children to share any experiences they have had at the airport and on an aeroplane and encourage them to name as many workers as they can.

After reading
Build upon children's curiosity and desire to explore
- With children, look at the photos of the cockpit and discuss how pilots use different instruments of measurement. Some children will be interested to learn that an altimeter tells the distance the plane is off the ground and an airspeed indicator tells the pilot how fast they are flying through the air.
- In the gym or on the playground, demonstrate the importance of an air traffic controller by having one child be an "air traffic controller" while other children wait for directions to "take off". First have the controller count to 10 between telling individual children to "take off" (walking a single line). Discuss how the distance between "planes" changes depending on when the controller tells them to take off.

24